Church Basics

Understanding
Church Discipline

Author and Series Editor Jonathan Leeman

PUBLISHING GROUP
Nashville, Tennessee

Copyright © 2016 by Jonathan Leeman and 9Marks
All rights reserved.
Printed in the United States of America

978-1-4336-8891-1

Published by B&H Publishing Group
Nashville, Tennessee

Dewey Decimal Classification: 262
Subject Heading: CHURCH DISCIPLINE \ CHURCH MEMBERSHIP \
DOCTRINAL THEOLOGY

Unless otherwise noted, all Scripture is from the Holman Christian
Standard Bible (HCSB), copyright © 1999, 2000, 2002, 2003, 2009
by Holman Bible Publishers. Used by permission.

Also used: New International Version®, NIV® copyright ©1973, 1978, 1984,
2011 by Biblica, Inc.® Used by permission. All rights reserved worldwide.

Also used: English Standard Version (ESV), copyright © 2001 by Crossway
Bibles, a publishing ministry of Good News Publishers.

1 2 3 4 5 6 7 8 • 20 19 18 17 16

CONTENTS

"A simple, tender book for the members of the church as
they undertake some of their most difficult and important,
neglected and yet significant work." —Mark Dever

CHURCH BASICS SERIES PREFACE

The Christian life is the churched life. This basic biblical conviction informs every book in the Church Basics series.

That conviction in turn affects how each author treats his topic. For instance, *Understanding the Lord's Supper* maintains that the Lord's Supper is not a private, mystical act between you and Jesus. It is a meal around the family table in which you commune with Christ and Christ's people. *Understanding the Great Commission* contends that the Great Commission is not a license to head into the nations as Jesus' witness all by oneself. It is a charge given to the whole church to be fulfilled by the whole church. *Understanding the Congregation's Authority* observes that the authority of the church rests not only with the leaders, but with the entire assembly. Every member has a job to do, including you.

Every book is written *for* the average church member, and this is a crucial point. If the Christian life is a churched life, then you, a baptized believer and church member, have a responsibility to understand these basic topics. Just as Jesus charges you with promoting and protecting his gospel message, so he charges you with promoting and protecting his gospel people, the church. These books will explain how.

You are like a shareholder in Christ's gospel ministry corporation. And what do good shareholders do? They study their company, study the market, and study the competition. They want the most out of their investment. You, Christian, have invested your whole life in the gospel. The purpose of the series, then, is to help you maximize the health and kingdom profitability of your local congregation for God's glorious gospel ends.

Are you ready to get to work?

Jonathan Leeman
Series Editor

Books in Church Basic series

Understanding the Great Commission, Mark Dever
Understanding Baptism, Bobby Jamieson
Understanding the Lord's Supper, Bobby Jamieson
Understanding the Congregation's Authority, Jonathan Leeman
Understanding Church Discipline, Jonathan Leeman
Understanding Church Leadership, Mark Dever

For further instruction on these topics from these authors (B&H):

Don't Fire Your Church Members: The Case for Congregationalism, Jonathan Leeman

Going Public: Why Baptism Is Required for Church Membership, Bobby Jamieson

Baptist Foundations: Church Government for an Anti-Institutional Age, Mark Dever and Jonathan Leeman, editors

Preach: Theology Meets Practice, Mark Dever and Greg Gilbert

The Church: The Gospel Made Visible, Mark Dever

CHAPTER 1

You Have a Job to Do

If you have children, you have probably felt that leaden thud in the gut—"ugh"—when you realize it's time to discipline one of your kids. Right up until that moment, you have done everything you could to give her a way out of trouble (I only have daughters). You let her explain any extenuating circumstances. You have second-guessed whether your instructions were clear. But now the facts overtake you like a foul stench: she is guilty. Your precious, heart-enrapturing little Cinderella flagrantly disobeyed you. Or lied. Or nailed her sister in the face. And now love requires you to discipline her. Ugh.

> For the LORD disciplines the one He loves, just as a father, the son he delights in. (Prov. 3:12)

> The one who will not use the rod hates his son, but the one who loves him disciplines him diligently. (Prov. 13:24)

> Discipline your children, for in that there is hope; do not be a willing party to their death. (Prov. 19:18 NIV)

Striking verses, no? Failing to discipline our children is hating them. It is forsaking hope for them. It is being a willing party to their death.

Love disciplines.

Tragically, turn on the news and there is a decent chance you will hear a story about a horribly abusive parent. And such stories can cause us to back away from the idea of discipline. Would that Jesus return and end such abuses! Yet in the meantime we know we cannot throw out the baby with the bathwater. It remains our job as parents to discipline. We do it for love and life.

> For a command is a lamp, teaching is a light, and corrective discipline is the way to life. (Prov. 6:23)

You Have a Job to Do

Just as it is a parent's job to discipline his or her children, so it is your job, Christian, to participate in the discipline of your church. Did you know that? This is as basic to being a Christian and a church member as it is for a parent to discipline a child. It is part and parcel of following Jesus. Listen to how Jesus puts it:

> "If your brother sins against you, go and rebuke him in private. If he listens to you, you have won your brother. But if he won't listen, take one or two more with you, so that by the testimony of two or three witnesses every fact may be established. If he pays no attention to them, tell the church. But if he doesn't pay attention even to the church, let him be like an unbeliever and a tax collector to you." (Matt. 18:15–17)

To whom is Jesus talking in this passage? He is talking to *you*, assuming you are a Christian and a church member. Jesus, the one with all authority in heaven and earth, is tasking *you* with this job. This is *your* job description. It's not just for the pastors or elders. It's not just for the old Christians or mature Christians. This is a job for *you*.

> "The wounds of a friend are trustworthy, but the kisses of an enemy are excessive." (Prov. 27:6)

If a brother sins against you, you are tasked with addressing him. This is what it means to be a true friend.

If your friend listens, praise God. Your job is done. If he does not listen, then it's your job to bring a few others. Other eyes and ears help to make sure you are seeing straight. If you all agree, and if your friend remains stuck in his sin, then you may need to bring the matter to the whole church (with the help

> "Without guidance, people fall, but with many counselors there is deliverance." (Prov. 11:14)

of the elders). And if he does not listen to the church, then you are to treat him like an unbeliever who no longer belongs to the church.

Speaking of this last step, who is the "you" in the concluding command, "let him be like an unbeliever and a tax collector to you"? Is it a plural *you,* as if to say, "treat him like an unbeliever y'all"?

If we had super-powered Greek-reading glasses on, we could see that behind the English word "you" is a singular Greek "you." It means: you. You are to treat as a non-Christian this fellow church member who doesn't repent. So is every other "you" in your church. You become personally and corporately responsible for this work of exclusion. Just as it is your job to confront, so it is your job to participate in the corporate exclusion.

Some churches involve only the pastors in these last couple of steps. The elders or pastors are said to stand-in for the church. So "tell it to the church" is interpreted as "tell it to the elders." Of course, that's not what the text says. That's not how the first readers would have understood the word *church* there. And it interrupts the ascending numeric trajectory of the text: from one, to two or three, to the whole assembly. Clearly, Jesus treats the gathered church as the final court of appeal in matters of discipline.

No doubt, this passage requires a few asterisks and some fine print. We will come to those later. The simple point now is, you have a job to do. It is to participate in the discipline of the church.

This may be hard to hear. Maybe Matthew 18 elicits an "ugh" of its own. Doesn't Jesus tell us elsewhere not "to judge"? Indeed, he does in Matthew 7. But whatever Jesus means in Matthew 7, he does not mean to hinder you from this job assignment given a few chapters later.

Notice that Paul, too, calls us to rescue our fellow church members from sin:

> Brothers, if someone is caught in any wrongdoing, you who
> are spiritual should restore such a person with a gentle spirit,
> watching out for yourselves so you also won't be tempted.
> Carry one another's burdens; in this way you will fulfill the law
> of Christ. (Gal. 6:1–2)

By "spiritual," Paul doesn't mean mature. He means walking by the fruits of the Spirit as opposed to the fruits of the flesh (5:16–26). He is talking to everyone who would presume to be a fruit-bearing Christian and church member. If *anyone* is caught in sin, *you* who intend to walk by the Spirit should work to restore this person. This is one way to carry a person's burdens and to fulfill the law of Christ. It is acting like a Christian. The flip-side is obvious: refusing to confront brothers and sisters in their sin is to forsake the law of Christ. It's to wander off Christ's path.

What Is Church Discipline?

What is church discipline? The broad answer is to say it is correcting sin in the church. Notice how the book of Proverbs, speaking about the idea of discipline broadly, places discipline and correction in parallel:

> Whoever loves *discipline* loves knowledge,
> but one who hates *correction* is stupid. (Prov. 12:1, italics added)

To discipline is to correct, to rebuke, to warn. Such correction can occur privately and informally, as when a friend at church remarked how selfish I could be. That was a small act of discipline. Hopefully

I learned from it. But once in a while such correction becomes formal and public. This involves telling the church and—if a person still does not repent after the church is told—removing him or her from membership. This very last step of removal is sometimes called "excommunication."

Roman Catholicism has used the word *excommunication* to describe the process of removing people from church membership *and* salvation—as if the church could deny salvation. Among Protestants, excommunication simply means removing members from membership in the local church and the Lord's Table (a person is ex-communioned). It is *not* saying the person is assuredly a non-Christian. We don't have Holy Spirit-eyes to see souls, after all. Rather, it is a church's way of saying, "We can no longer lend our corporate kingdom name and credibility to affirming that this individual is a Christian. Instead, we will treat this person as a non-Christian."

In this book I will use both the words *discipline* and *excommunication*, the latter especially to refer to that final step.

People accept the idea of discipline in other areas of life. Our coaches pushed us to discipline our bodies to prepare for a race. Our teachers pushed us to discipline our minds in preparation for tests. Then our teachers disciplined us by grading those tests. And in these other domains of

> "Apply yourself to discipline and listen to words of knowledge." (Prov. 23:12)

life, we know that correction brings growth. If you want your rose bush to grow, you trim it.

In fact, I remember the first time I took a pair of trimmers to a rose bush in my front yard. It didn't feel right. It made me nervous. "Am I really supposed to cut these branches off? Won't this hurt the plant?" But I went ahead and trimmed—on faith. A year later—lo and behold—the bush overflowed with blossoms.

People also accept the idea of discipline in other organizations. There was no public outcry when the United States Anti-Doping Agency stripped Lance Armstrong of his seven Tour de France titles after determining that he had won them through illegal doping. People likewise accept that lawyers who tamper with the evidence should be disbarred. And doctors who prescribe illegal drugs should lose their medical license. And building contractors or electricians or plumbers who violate building codes to save a buck should be fined and possibly imprisoned.

Yet when it comes to *church* discipline, we feel differently.

No One Opposes Discipline, but Few Practice It

I have "enjoyed" the strange providence of writing and speaking about the peculiar topic of church discipline (among other topics, gratefully) for about a decade now. Interestingly, I have never once heard a Christian argue that church discipline was unbiblical. The biblical case for church discipline is just too clear. It is difficult to deny.

Historian Greg Wills makes a similar observation in his fascinating book *Democratic Religion*. He describes how common church discipline was in Baptist churches up until the American Civil War. Then the practice started to fade away. No theologian argued against discipline, Wills says. No movement of churches rallied against it. It simply backed into the shadows. Other things grabbed churches' attention, like remaining financially solvent, increasing their market share, or even reforming society at large (and not just themselves).

My sense is that most pastors today admit church discipline is biblical. But few churches practice it. No matter where I have addressed this topic, people find an excuse to avoid obeying Jesus and Paul's instructions above. South Africans say it doesn't work in a tribal culture like theirs. Brazilians observe that people's families are too tight-knit. Native Hawaiians suggest it's too confrontational for their live-and-let-live ethic. East Asianers say it doesn't work in a shame culture. And Americans are concerned about getting sued. Everyone has an excuse.

I have news for such excuse-makers: you're not different. There is no culture in the history of the world for whom "church discipline" has felt natural and comfortable. The world's first act of church discipline, when God evicted Adam and Eve from the garden, was hardly a comfortable affair.

Speaking less globally and more locally, discipline is a difficult matter for any number of reasons.

- Church members are not accustomed to being held accountable for their sin.
- Pastors are sinful too.
- You live, in some cases, with doubt about whether discipline is the best action.
- You wonder if you have done all that you could reasonably do to reclaim the offender first.
- The person can completely misunderstand the intent of the discipline and get angry, incite rebellion, or become resentful and drop out of contact.
- Who wants confrontation?!

The list goes on.

I remember one occasion when a close friend of my family explained that she was involved in a particular kind of sin. I won't get into the details, but it was 95 percent clear to me that what she was doing was sin. And it was 0 percent clear to her. I consulted with several others. Everyone agreed it was sin, and it was significant. My fellow elders suggested it could result in her removal from the church. My wife and I, of course, loathed this possibility. She was a young Christian and a sweet friend.

So we pleaded with her over several weeks. For several evenings, I woke up in the middle of the night with a churning stomach, not something typical of me. I usually have no difficulty sleeping. And that 5 percent of doubt made me second-guess the whole process.

Ultimately, she repented. Thank the Lord! Yet the process was tough. It temporarily strained our friendship. It was emotionally taxing. And it risked provoking her to abandon our church.

Today, however, there is no doubt in my mind that it was the right thing to do. She had been broadcasting to the world that Christians engage in that particular sin. And she was endangering her own walk with the Lord. Yet the temporary sacrifice she made by forsaking that sin is doing her eternal good.

Purpose of This Book

The purpose of this book is to help you, the average Christian and church member, grab hold of this job responsibility of yours. I have already written one book on the topic: *Church Discipline: How the Church Protects the Name of Jesus.* If that book is like flying an airplane over the topic and was written more for pastors, letting them look down on the whole forest, this book is more like a walk through the woods and has been written for church members. My goal is to help you do your job as a member.

And it's important that you do your job, perhaps more so than ever. Western culture increasingly pushes against Christianity. Nominal Christianity is withering. Christians need to know who "they" are. And the world needs to know who "we" are. Discipline helps to draw the line between church and world. It clarifies the witness of the church and its power as a distinct society and counterculture.

Not only that, the Bible—that counterintuitive and countercultural book of ours—contests that God disciplines us "for our benefit, so that we can share His holiness." It continues: "No discipline seems enjoyable at the time, but painful. Later on, however, it yields the fruit of peace and righteousness to those who have been trained by it" (Heb. 12:10b–11).

Do you want the fruit of peace and righteousness for yourself and your church? If not, never mind discipline. If you do want to taste this fruit and to help others do the same, keep reading.

> LORD, happy is the man You discipline and teach from Your law. (Ps. 94:12)

CHAPTER 2

Getting Ready for Work

When I was in seminary, a guy in my dormitory referred to himself as the "Heresy Hunter." More recently I heard about a Bible college student who started a discussion group called "That's-The-Truth-Now-Deal-With-It." And then there are the bloggers who self-style as guardians of the sheep, and whose every post consists of labeling someone a wolf.

Needless to say, these kinds of people—call them snipers or grenade throwers—are not the ones you want leading a church through the activities of discipline. It's always easy to shoot from a distance or to lob an accusation.

> A fool's displeasure is known at once, but whoever ignores an insult is sensible. (Prov. 12:16)

> Stay away from a foolish man; you will gain no knowledge from his speech. (Prov. 14:7)

> A fool gives full vent to his anger, but a wise man holds it in check. (Prov. 29:11)

Most of us, however, probably err in the opposite direction. We are more likely to start a group called "That's-The-Truth-But-I'm-NOT-Going-To-Say-It." Or "That's-The Truth-But-I'm-

Going-To-Gossip-About-It-To-Someone-Else." Then we let wolves go on as wolves. Fear of what people think keeps us from speaking. We forsake the opportunity to do real good, as Proverbs would advise:

> He who gives an honest answer gives a kiss on the lips. (Prov. 24:26)

> A word spoken at the right time is like gold apples on a silver tray. (Prov. 25:11)

> A ruler can be persuaded through patience, and a gentle tongue can break a bone. (Prov. 25:15)

Whether you find confrontation easy or difficult, erring in one direction or the other, we all need help. We need the right mental framework and the right posture of heart.

Here's a super-clear example: Jesus tells us to take the log out of our own eye before we take the speck out of someone else's (Matt. 7:3–5). If your heart is unwilling to consider the possibility that your eye has a log in it, you probably should not call attention to the specks in the eyes of others, *even if you are right about any given speck*.

What I would like to do in this chapter, then, is to offer five characteristics of the right mental framework and heart posture for discipline.

What Is the Gospel?

The good news is that Jesus lived the perfect life we should have lived, paid the penalty for sin in his death that we should pay, and rose from the dead defeating sin and death. He now offers salvation to all who repent and believe and promises to come again and restore all things for those who are his.

1. You Trust the Power of the Gospel to Change

Sometimes people are confused by the idea of church discipline. Isn't the good news of Christianity that we can be saved from our sin through

Jesus' death and resurrection by faith alone, and not by works? If we are saved by grace through faith alone, how can we be removed from the church for bad works?

The gospel does justify us by faith and not by works. But the faith that justifies *works*. The Holy Spirit of God really does change people. Christ paid the penalty for sin on the cross. He rose from the dead conquering sin's hold, death, and was declared the firstborn of a new creation. Now he ushers his people into this new creation and new race. He causes them to be born again. Paul therefore remarks:

> How can we who died to sin still live in it? . . . Therefore we
> were buried with Him by baptism into death, in order that, just
> as Christ was raised from the dead by the glory of the Father,
> so we too may walk in a new way of life. (Rom. 6:2, 4)

Repentance and faith, two sides of the same coin, characterize this new humanity. Therefore we should expect and begin looking for signs of repentance in a believer's life. The trees in a person's life might remain mostly bare, the streams largely covered with ice. But the signs of spring can't be missed: the first buds, the sound of trickling water, the glimpse of a fawn.

That's why Paul tells the Corinthians, "Test yourselves to see if you are in the faith. Examine yourselves. Or do you yourselves not recognize that Jesus Christ is in you?—unless you fail the test" (2 Cor. 13:5). This may not be the favorite verse of individualistic Western Christians, but Paul clearly believes that having Jesus Christ in us by his Spirit will result in changed lives. And those differences can be proven through testing, through examining. To paraphrase John Newton, I'm not what I should be, but by God's grace I am not what I once was. Every Christian should be able to say that.

Christians will sin. But it's the fight against sin that shows them to be Christians.

2. You Are Convinced Holiness Is Better than Unholiness

Church discipline exists because God is holy, and because his holiness is good.

Admittedly, we often don't like the sound of holiness, even if we as church members give lip service to it. Part of us still wants what the world offers, like looking at the salad menu and quietly hungering for a hamburger and fries.

But church discipline begins with the assumption that God is better. God is better than what he has created. God is better than perversions of what he has created—or sin. God is better than everything. Therefore nothing is better than being consecrated to God. And this is holiness—being consecrated or set apart to God.

> ### What Is Holiness?
> Being separated *from* sin and being consecrated *to* God and God's glory.

It's difficult to imagine how someone could *properly* pursue church discipline apart from the conviction that God's holiness is better. You shouldn't pursue discipline for vindictive reasons. You shouldn't pursue it to punish a person. You shouldn't do it because, like Inspector Javert in *Les Misérables*, you want to impose your vision of justice on the universe. You do it because you know how good God is, and a person's unrepentant sin separates him or her from his goodness, and—oh, please God!—you want the person to know this goodness. It's like wanting good things for your children, but watching their foolish decisions keep them from enjoying the goodness.

To put it another way, discipline should grow out of longing. Longing for holiness. Longing that God's will be done on earth as it is in heaven. Longing for the better.

In other words . . .

3. You Love with God's Love, Not the World's Love

Pursuing discipline for the sake of holiness is pursuing it for the sake of love. To love is to want what is best for the beloved. And God is always best. He is best for the person in sin, best for ourselves, best for our churches. So true love wants holiness for the beloved.

True love and holiness are inseparable. The world denies this. In fact, it cannot conceive of it. Ever since the Serpent slid into the garden, the world has believed that respecting a person's independence best shows love. So when God says, "You will enjoy and experience the greatest of all loves by consecrating your life to me," the world takes offense. It steps backward, eyes wide with shock, and yells, "How dare you be so self-centered and unloving, God!"

But Jesus says, "If anyone loves Me, he will keep My word" (John 14:23).

And Jesus says, "If you keep My commands you will remain in My love, just as I have kept My Father's commands and remain in His love" (John 15:10).

> ### What Is Biblical Love?
> Possessing affection for the good of another, knowing that the greatest good is the holy God.

And John says, "For this is what love for God is: to keep His commands" (1 John 5:3a).

These are not the words of a killjoy. These are the words of someone who knows that God's commands are good, because God is good, and that joy awaits those who walk in the ways of God. John continues, "Now His commands are not a burden, because whatever has been born of God conquers the world" (3b–4). Our worldly concepts of love cause us to close in on ourselves—our desires, our feelings, our sense of self. But God's love turns us outward and makes us world conquerors—if only we would open our eyes to the hugeness and majesty and glory of God, and then walk in his ways.

It is not love to let a crumble of rock floating in space think it's the sun. And it is not love to let a creature carry on uninterrupted in rebellion against the Creator.

Is a prophet loving who says "Peace, peace" when there is no peace?

So as you prepare for the work of discipline, ask yourself, why are you considering it? Are you convinced that God is best? That God is love? That the holiness of God calls us to a life filled with satisfaction and joy? That Christ is better than anything this world offers? Do you want your fellow member who has been deceived by sin to experience God more than sin? If so, you're off to the right start.

4. You Trust That Obedience to God Is True Freedom

Some sinful desires root deeper than others. A man learned anger from his father. A woman experiences same-sex attraction. A son struggles with jealously and contempt toward a long-favored brother.

By saying the sin roots deeper, I mean it stretches farther back into the shadowy cave of personal history than the eyes of memory can reach. It feels like it's always been there. It's not a bad habit recently picked up from a friend that can be defeated with a concerted push of mental effort. It feels necessary, unchangeable, natural. Push and push and push, but it keeps springing back into place. The sin must be "me," part of my identity.

How often have the saints been discouraged by these sins that won't seem to die—sins they are tempted to name Inevitable!

The world looks at these deepest desires, however, and pleads for the freedom to indulge them: "This desire is you, and it is good. Express yourself." Freedom, to the world's way of thinking, is being unrestrained to indulge your desires. And one of the greatest moral values in the West today is this kind of freedom. Indeed, to love someone is to set him or her free to these desires that run deep.

The Bible, too, values freedom, but it knows true freedom is found elsewhere. It values not freedom *from* restraint, but freedom *to—to* obey God and *to* imitate his character. "You will know the truth, and the truth will set you free" (John 8:32). The freedom of the world, ironically, the Bible calls slavery. The Bible says we are ruled like slaves by our fallen desires (see Rom. 6 and 7). To say a person is free to follow his fallen desires is like telling a slave he is free to obey the master who would destroy him—only that master is his own flesh.

True freedom is being born again to want what God wants. You begin to want God's truth, God's character, God's ways, God's delights—the very things for which we are designed. God's pleasures become your pleasures. Biblical freedom is the freedom that a trained dancer experiences in the perfect pirouette, that the jazz pianist enjoys in a mixture of structure and improvisation, that an architect who has mastered engineering and geometry enjoys as his pencil lines push a skyscraper heavenward.

Biblical freedom, in other words, is the freedom to create the goodness and beauty that every master craftsman has learned through years of training and discipline. Church discipline works slowly and carefully for this kind of freedom. It trains

> **What Is Biblical Freedom?**
> Possessing the desire and the ability to do the will of God.

the born-again mind and heart in the craft of living by God's Word and according to his character. Is there anything more beautiful than a life that images the kindness, love, goodness, righteousness, wisdom, and compassion of God?

The point, then, is not that the corrections of our fellow church members will always root out the weeds of sin that are planted deep, at least not in this life. The point is that we begin the weeding or the training for holiness together. We must not be hoodwinked by the false freedom of giving into sinful desire. For as *natural* as a sinful desire feels, Christians rely upon the *supernatural* to change and to re-create, piece by piece now and wholesale then.

However deep our natural desires go, God's Spirit reaches deeper still (1 Cor. 2:10–16). "Therefore," says Paul, "I do not run like one who runs aimlessly or box like one beating the air. Instead, I discipline my body and bring it under strict control" (1 Cor. 9:26–27). And he did this even while a thorn in the flesh (a temptation?) was never removed (2 Cor. 12:7–9). In the church we do this together and for one another. Church discipline means team training.

You are off to a right start in the work of discipline, I said, if you long for holiness and are motivated by love. Now let me add this: your goal in correcting sin must also be freedom. Your message to the person caught in sin is always, "Christ has liberated us to be free. Stand firm then and don't submit again to a yoke of slavery" (Gal. 5:1).

At some point, of course, we discipline not for the purposes of training, but for the purpose of redemption (1 Cor. 5:5). When the final step of discipline is reached, and a person is excommunicated from the church, we are saying that it appears he or she needs to be redeemed. Our hope is that this final step of removal will wake up the person to this fact. It is as if we have been standing for months on the edge of the slave plantation, begging the slave to abandon his chains. But he persists in his refusal. So finally we turn and walk away, hoping that, if nothing else, the sight of us leaving will induce him to abandon his slavery and follow.

5. You Prize Wisdom More than Airing Your Opinions, Efficiency, or Winning

Suppose a friend says something that offends you. Or suppose you are talking to a Christian brother whose marriage is troubled, and you sense that it's his fault. Or imagine you perceive a growing hardness of heart in a Christian sister based on pattern of sarcastic and disdainful remarks about others. There is a certain kind of person, says Proverbs, who will observe each one of these situations and jump into the fray too quickly.

> The one who gives an answer before he listens—this is foolishness and disgrace for him. (Prov. 18:13)

> A fool does not delight in understanding, but only wants to show off his opinions. (Prov. 18:2)

The fool wants to look good. He enjoys correcting because he thinks it makes him appear superior. He thinks it shows everyone that he has mastered the matter, transcended the trouble. So he raises his eyebrow and feels himself justified.

But wisdom walks, doesn't rush:

> A patient person shows great understanding, but a quick-tempered one promotes foolishness. (Prov. 14:29)

> A wise man will listen and increase his learning, and a discerning man will obtain guidance. (Prov. 1:5)

A person who prizes wisdom understands that life is complicated. There is a time you should not answer a fool in his foolishness (Prov. 26:4). And there is a time you *should* answer a fool in his foolishness (v. 5). There is a time to tear down and time to build, a time to throw stones and a time to gather them, a time to embrace and a time to avoid embracing, a time to be silent and a time to speak, a time to love and a time to hate, a time for war and a time for peace (Eccl. 3:3, 5, 7–8). The wise always pay attention to what time it is. There is a time to correct a fellow member and a time not to correct. Going back to the opening illustrations, maybe you've misunderstood your friend's offensive words. Or maybe it's less that husband's fault than you think it is. Or maybe that sister's heart isn't growing hard; she's feeling neglected and hurt.

Sometimes churches, for efficiency's sake, establish church discipline policies: "under circumstances 'x,' we will proceed to church discipline." But lest we bind ourselves where Scripture does not bind us, such policies need to be softened with a big "ordinarily": "we will ordinarily proceed . . ." Wisdom understands, as one old Greek philosopher put it, that you never step into the same river twice. Wisdom therefore insists on asking lots of questions. Considering extenuating circumstances. Listening for multiple layers of explanation. Giving the benefit of the doubt.

> ### What Is Biblical Wisdom?
> The *posture* of recognizing that the universe is God's, as well as the *skill* of successfully navigating the complexities of an orderly yet sometimes unpredictable, even unjust world.

The wise exercise sensitivity and compassion. They know wisdom comes from God, not from themselves: "For the LORD gives wisdom; from His mouth come knowledge and understanding" (Prov. 2:6). They cannot expect more from others than they expect from themselves. And this makes them patient, not anxious. They know understanding comes slowly, just as the child takes years to learn from the father. They cannot force the outcome but must wait for the Lord. A person who practices discipline must be patient—oh so patient.

The wise also love wisdom more than winning. They start with questions, not accusations. They listen. And they are willing to change course mid-conversation as new knowledge comes to light, unafraid to admit error. Ego isn't captain of the conversation.

A person who is more concerned with winning or reputation, however, does not listen. Once the confrontational conversation begins, there's no turning back. The person has to win. He employs evidence and explanations to confirm his biases and prejudgments. There is almost a sense in which we can say that the person who is more concerned with winning has imbalanced scales, scales which tilt to make him look good.

Differing weights are detestable to the Lord, and dishonest
scales are unfair. (Prov. 20:23)

Keep the rules without prejudging, doing nothing from par-
tiality. (1 Tim. 5:21 esv)

So as you prepare for the work of discipline, ask yourself, have
you already prejudged the situation and already rendered a verdict?
Or are you interested in seeking understanding? Are you able to begin
conversations by asking genuine questions and not only leading questions? Do you recognize that wisdom comes from God, not from your
vast store of experience and oh-so-righteous living? Finally, do you
recognize that we all grow in wisdom slowly, and that includes the
person caught in sin? Their first reaction might be defensive. But wait
and watch. See if the heart begins to soften. You, too, sometimes take
time to discover the truth, remember? I suspect I can confirm that fact
with your mother.

A Culture of Meaningful Membership

Like marriage, church discipline can be done poorly. Too often it
is. And one of the easiest ways to ensure you will pursue or be pursued
in discipline poorly is to keep everyone in your church at arm's length
relationally. Don't spend time with people outside of the weekly gathering. Never invest in others or learn about their life experiences. If you
do, don't confess your own sin or be transparent. Live on the surface
and keep your relationships shallow. Don't inconvenience yourself for
anyone. Then, after several years of doing that, start correcting people.
See how the discipline goes then.

In fact, church discipline works best in a church culture marked by
encouragement and love. Henry Drummond wrote,

You will find, if you think for a moment, that the people who
influence you are people who believe in you. In an atmosphere

of suspicion men shrivel up; but in that atmosphere they
expand, and find encouragement and educative fellowship.[1]

We most quickly receive the corrections of the people who have demonstrated their love for us over time. Is your church involvement characterized by persistent demonstrations of love? If you hold positions of authority in the church, are you known for using your authority to build up, not tear down? If not, maybe put this book down, and pick it up again in a year.

CHAPTER 3

Your Place of Work

It's important to be a church member. In fact, it may be more important now than at any time in the history of the West.

Formerly, everyone from your school friends, to your teachers, to your doctor, to the owner of the general store, to the mayor, to your colleagues at work probably called themselves Christians. Whether or not they were is another story. But their belief about their beliefs made it easier for you to go along, get along as a Christian. Their values basically reinforced yours: work hard, keep sex in marriage, and give the minister a smiling handshake on the way out the church door on Sunday. In such times there might have been hypocrites aplenty. The nominal Christians might have outnumbered the true. But few newspaper editorialists and Hollywood producers made war on your basic moral principles. They wouldn't call you a hater for believing what Christians have always believed.

Times have sure changed, in some ways for the better, in some ways for the worse. Civil rights for African Americans is good. The end of people believing they are Christians when they aren't is good. But in other ways it's becoming harder for a Christian to live and believe like a Christian, not that Jesus promised otherwise. Didn't he say something about having trouble in this world?

Americans like to think of themselves as independent thinkers. But none of us really are. We wear the clothes our friends wear. We laugh at the same television shows as our friends. We spend money on the same vacation spots as our friends. We broadly call right and wrong what our friends call right and wrong. We are all influenced by the people we choose to be around.

With times being what they are, then, it's more important than ever before to have a church around you. You will have to swim upstream in this world to survive as a Christian. Think you can do that alone?

What Is the Local Church?

In the previous chapters, I said that Jesus assigned all of us who are Christians with participating in the discipline of the church. And then we thought about the mental framework and heart posture necessary for such work. Let's take a moment now to think about our actual place of work: the church where you are a member. It's more important than ever before to be a member, I just said. But what exactly is the church?

There are so many ways to answer that question. The Greek word for *church* roughly translates as "called out ones." The Bible refers to the church as the people of God, the body of Christ, the temple of the Spirit, a holy nation, a royal priesthood, the flock, the pillar and foundation of truth, and so much more. Jesus identified his very self with the church (Acts 9:4). We could think about any of these descriptions for hours.

Yet join me for just a second in Dupont Circle in Washington, D.C. If we start walking northwest on Massachusetts Avenue, we immediately pass on our left the Embassy of Portugal followed by the Embassy of Indonesia. A block up on our right is the Embassy of India. And then back on the left side another block up are the embassies of Luxembourg, Togo, Sudan, The Bahamas, Ireland, and Romania. Whoops, across the street on the right side we almost missed the embassies of Turkmenistan and Greece. On and on Mass Ave goes:

Latvia, South Korea, Burkina Faso, Haiti, Croatia, Kyrgyz Republic, Madagascar, Paraguay, Malawi, and so on.

Embassy Row, it's called, and it is amazing. Out in front of each embassy you will see the flag of each country flying. Walk inside and you will hear the language of another people. Join them for a dinner and taste the things that grow and feed in their national soil. Then sneak into the ambassador's office and eavesdrop on the nation's diplomatic business. Not that I've ever made it past the exterior flags!

But these aren't the only embassies in Washington, D.C. There are embassies of another kind: the gospel-preaching local churches. The local church, too, represents another kingdom. You won't find that kingdom across any ocean. Christ's king-

> ### What Is a Church?
> A group of Christians who jointly identify as followers of Jesus through regularly gathering in his name, preaching the gospel, and celebrating the ordinances.

dom is waiting for us at the end of history, only its citizens have begun to appear in history now. They gather on the Lord's Day, the first day of the week. They proclaim the saving and ruling message of Christ the King. They raise their flag through baptism, and their national cuisine comes in a wafer and a cup.

Yes, I am speaking metaphorically when referring to the gathered local church as an embassy. But that is what a local church is. We are citizens of heaven, say the authors of the New Testament (Phil. 3:20; Heb. 8:11; cp. Eph. 2:19; 1 Pet. 1:1). We are the people of Christ's kingdom and a holy nation, living in the midst of this world's nations. And the gathering of a church is this kind of embassy, or outpost, or colony, or Christ's kingdom. Together we bow to another Lord. We possess an otherworldly culture: poverty of spirit, mourning our sin, meekness, hungering and thirsting for righteousness, mercy, purity of heart, peacemaking, and even a willingness to be persecuted. Our talk is different. Our manners are strange. We even do unaccountable things with our money, like give it away. And then there's our ambassadorial business: calling others to be reconciled to our king (2 Cor. 5:16–21).

In other words, the nations of the world should be able to walk into one of our gatherings and say, "These people don't act like us. Where do they come from?" They should be amazed by the wisdom of our God on display through our unity (Eph. 3:10). They should envy our love (see John 13:34–35). And they should be tempted to praise God when they see our good deeds (Matt. 5:16; 1 Pet. 2:12).

Your local church and mine should indeed consist of the called out ones. We are the people of God, the dwelling place of his Spirit, and the body of his Son! We are otherworldly. And our gatherings, no matter where they happen, are like the embassies on Massachusetts Avenue in Washington, D.C., only stranger and more wonderful.

The Authority of the Local Church

What's more, the local church possesses the authority to speak in a special and formal kind of way for King Jesus. For instance, you might think of how the Indonesian Embassy in Washington can speak for the government of Indonesia more formally than can an Indonesian tourist walking the streets of Washington. Similarly, a gathered local church can make "official" declarations on behalf of heaven in a way that an individual Christian cannot. And church discipline depends upon the fact that the gathered church can make official declarations on behalf of Jesus and his rule in heaven.

I think Christians today have a hard time understanding this. It's hard just to understand—"What does it *mean* that a church can 'speak' for heaven in a way that I as a Christian cannot?" And it's hard to accept—"That can't be right, can it?"

I've written about this at length elsewhere, but let me try show you briefly in Matthew's Gospel where I'm getting this. To begin with, Matthew's Gospel is preoccupied with the question of who represents heaven on earth. Back in the garden of Eden, heaven and earth dwelled together. In Genesis 3, of course, they were torn apart. Matthew's Gospel begins, however, with John the Baptist and Jesus who show up announcing that the kingdom of heaven is at hand. Jesus goes on to describe who will possess the kingdom of heaven and inherit the earth. He then tells his disciples to pray for the heavenly Father's will to be done on earth as it is in heaven. And he tells them to store up their treasures in heaven, not on earth (Matt. 3:2; 4:17; 5:3, 5; 6:9–10, 20). On and on Matthew's Gospel goes, mentioning heaven or the kingdom of heaven 73 times. The Gospel concludes with Jesus saying that the Father has granted him all authority in heaven and on earth (28:18). Heaven and earth might not be entirely together again, but they are united under Jesus' rule. Jesus represents heaven!

Yet that's not all. In Matthew 16, Jesus gives the apostles something he calls "the keys of the kingdom," and then he gives those keys to the local church in Matthew 18. And he says these keys bind on earth what's bound in heaven and loose on earth what's loosed in heaven (Matt. 16:19; 18:18). What could that mean?

Just as Jesus affirms Peter and Peter's confession in Matthew 16, it means that the gathered church has the authority to affirm the *what* and the *who* of the gospel—*what* is a true gospel confession and *who* is a true gospel confessor. Sort of like this:

> Hear ye, hear ye, oh nations of the earth. We hereby declare on behalf of God in heaven that Jesus *is* the crucified and resurrected Messiah. *That* is the gospel message. We also declare that *these people* are citizens of his heavenly city. And you, nations of the earth, should regard this message as a heavenly message, and you should regard these people as heaven's citizens.

Or like this: "That is *not* heaven's message, and that is *not* a heavenly citizen."

In other words, Matthew 16 and 18 give local churches the authority to speak for Jesus and so speak for heaven. Churches do this by articulating their statements of faith and making people members—or removing those members.

What's helpful to recognize, I think, is that when Matthew's Gospel talks about the kingdom of heaven, it's not so much talking about a place. Rather, it's talking about something like a legal system or a government ("your kingdom come, your will be done . . ."). The kingdom of heaven in Matthew's Gospel is the heavenly Father's legal system or government. To bind or loose in heaven, then, is to speak with ambassadorial authority on behalf of heaven's government. A person's status in a place called heaven does not change when churches bind or loose people. Rather, a person's status on earth changes. He or she becomes a member of a visible church on earth—maybe your church. Or he or she is removed from that membership. So says the body charged with speaking for heaven's government.

I already used the metaphor of an embassy to illustrate the nature of the church's authority. An embassy can speak for a government in a way individual citizens cannot speak (say, by giving you your passport). Another metaphor that might be helpful for illustration purposes is to think of what a judge does. When a judge says "guilty" or "not guilty," he speaks on behalf of a legal system or government. He doesn't make the law what it is. He doesn't make a person guilty or innocent. But the fact that he speaks on behalf of a legal system means that his declaration has real-world consequences: the defendant goes free or goes to prison. Likewise, when the gathered church speaks, it affirms a certain doctrine or practice as in accordance with the gospel or not; and it affirms a certain person as a gospel citizen or not; and there are real-world consequences: a local church is organized accordingly.

Of course churches can be mistaken in their assessment, just like parents and princes and judges can be mistaken in their judgments. Still, the church's job is to present planet Earth with heaven's word on the *who* and the *what* of the gospel. They declare who the members of

Christ's body are. The church's speech is both legal (representing the kingdom of Christ) and covenantal (representing the new covenant).

How does a church make these declarations? It does it through baptism and the Lord's Supper. Baptism is the sign that we belong to the new covenant and Christ's kingdom people, just like circumcision was the sign of the Abrahamic covenant. The Lord's Supper is our regu-

> **What Is Church Membership?**
> A covenant between believers whereby they affirm one another's professions of faith through the ordinances and agree to oversee one another's discipleship to Christ.

lar meal of remembrance, just like Passover was the meal of remembrance for Israel. The ordinances present the world with a picture of who the church's members are. They place a Jesus nametag on our chests.

If you didn't follow all of that, here is the long and short of it: The local church specially speaks for heaven. It baptizes people into the name of the Father, Son, and Spirit. It gathers in his name to represent him, his name, and his authority (Matt. 18:20; 28:19–20). Christians, when gathered together as local churches, possess an authority that each of us as individual Christians do not possess: to define ourselves as a group of Christ's kingdom people; to mutually affirm the gospel message that makes us Christians; and to affirm or recognize one another as believers. You can put it even more simply: a church has the authority to write its own statement of faith and to affirm its own membership rolls. An individual Christian, by definition, cannot do these things. It takes two or three people to agree over the gospel and one another's gospel professions to be a church, after all. You agreeing with yourself does not a church make!

You and Your Work Place

Now here is something truly remarkable: Jesus tasks *you* with holding the keys of the kingdom together with your gathered church.

For instance, this is exactly what Paul says to the members of the Corinthian church in a case of church discipline: "When you are assembled in the name of our Lord Jesus with my spirit and with the power of our Lord Jesus, turn that one over to Satan for the destruction of the flesh, so that his spirit may be saved in the Day of the Lord" (1 Cor. 5:4–5). He's not addressing the elders or pastors; he's addressing the members of the Corinthian church. And notice where he said these members should hand this man over to the kingdom of Satan: when they are assembled in the name of Jesus. It's there that Jesus' power is present.

In fact, your work as a church member doesn't begin in the church's gatherings, but with your fellow members throughout the week. We'll talk about that in coming chapters. Still, it's worth seeing that you participate in the work of this embassy or colony of heaven. It's as if you entered an embassy building to get your passport renewed, and they put you to work! You are now a part of the ambassadorial staff.

As a church member, you work for an embassy representing heaven. Did you realize that? Did your mother ever have such lofty ambitions for you?

It's the Christians who realize that this is the high calling of church membership who will be able to survive as the world fights against Christianity. As for those who try to live apart from the accountability and fellowship of a church, well, they might survive for a while in a hostile city. But many will just assimilate. If only they knew what strength and safe harbor they would find inside the embassy gates!

CHAPTER 4

A Description
of Your Work—Part 1

Stephen was a friend and occasional running partner of mine back in the late nineties. We would run from Capitol Hill where we both lived, past the Capitol building, down the National Mall, and then back. Sometimes we would grab a bite to eat afterward. Good scenery. Good company.

Both of us were single at the time, and as two single men the conversation would naturally gravitate toward dating relationships. Typically these conversations were not terribly noteworthy—the sort of stuff you'd expect from Christian guys in their twenties. Then on one particular day Stephen shared with me that he had begun to pursue a path of sexual sin. When I pressed him, he immediately conceded that the Bible said it was wrong. But in his heart he believed that God was okay with his activity.

I spoke with him a couple of times on the matter. Then I brought in another church member, Brad, who was also a friend of Stephen's. Stephen responded to Brad like he did to me: unmoved. Brad and I next brought the matter to our church's elders, who encountered the same response from Stephen. And the elders brought Stephen's situation finally to the whole congregation.

Stephen at this point attempted to resign his membership from the church. But the elders understood that people join the church with the consent of the church and exit with the consent of the church. Jesus

29

gave authority to the local church—we saw in the last chapter—to discipline its members. What good would this authority be if a person could simply short-circuit it by resigning?

There are legal matters to treat with care here (a church should be able to demonstrate "informed consent" with its membership processes). But theologically, keep in mind what church membership is from the church's side: it's the church's formal affirmation of your profession of faith, together with its commitment to oversee your discipleship. Without discipline, that affirmation and oversight is meaningless, which is to say, membership is meaningless. If a church cannot withdraw its affirmation, what good is the affirmation? For that affirmation and oversight to mean anything, the church needs to be able to "correct the record." That is what excommunication is: the church saying to the community, "We previously affirmed this person's profession, but we can no longer do that." So the individual might not like it, but the church has its own public relations problem to resolve when the individual under discipline tries to resign. In fact, an individual attempting to resign while under discipline is trying to coerce the whole church to make a public statement about the individual the church doesn't believe.

But the Bible doesn't say, "If he doesn't listen to the church, treat him as an unbeliever or tax collector . . . unless he resigns first. Then treat him as a Christian." When Stephen tried to resign, the church therefore withheld his resignation. After several further warnings, it formally excluded him from membership and participation in the Lord's Table as an act of excommunication.

Getting Started: Build Relationships

So how do you as an ordinary church member approach church discipline? The place to begin is to build relationships with your fellow church members. You have other reasons to build relationships, of course. But one of them is to help yourself and others train for righteousness.

A couple chapters ago I observed that correction works best when people know one another and trust one another. It's like all the marriage and parenting books say: give ten words of encouragement for every word of correction. The same principle applies to our relationships at church. I'm thinking of my friend Donald, whom I can barely pass in the hallway without getting some word of encouragement. Not only that, Donald is a friend. He knows me. Therefore, if he finds need to correct me for being an idiot, which I have been known to be once or twice, do you think he has enough change in his pocket to pay that toll? You bet he does. I trust him. And ninety-nine percent of the discipline in a church should occur right here: in comparatively easy encounters between friends who trust each other.

The way for you to get started in your job is not for you to know every member of your church. It's not for you to pretend to be an extrovert when you're an introvert. Rather, it is for you to slowly start building meaningful and spiritually deliberate relationships with other members—according to your emotional bandwidth.

Notice I said "spiritually deliberate." It's fine to talk about football or schooling options for your kids. Do that. But also strive to have conversations that build up and give grace (Eph. 4:29). Ask your friends what they thought about Sunday's sermon. Point out evidences of grace. Share testimonies. Confess sin. Talk about what God has been teaching you about himself.

If this kind of conversation is unusual in your church culture, such talk will feel uncomfortable at first. That's okay. Take it easy and don't push it. Still, little by little, patiently and winsomely, be a cultural change agent by talking about things that will matter for eternity.

The Work: Reconcile, Restore, Encourage Repentance

In chapter 1 I defined church discipline broadly as correcting sin and narrowly as removing someone from membership in the church.

You start with correction. And little by little, when necessary, you work your way to removal, which itself hopefully leads to restoration. That's the super broad outline of the job.

In other words, you are working for reconciliation, restoration, or repentance. These are overlapping categories. To work for one is to work for all. But it's worth looking at biblical passages that emphasize each.

Reconciliation. To begin with, your job is to work for reconciliation. Sin divides. And the church should be united. Jesus teaches,

> "If your brother sins against you, go and rebuke him in private. If he listens to you, you have won your brother. But if he won't listen, take one or two more with you, so that by the testimony of two or three witnesses every fact may be established. If he pays no attention to them, tell the church. But if he doesn't pay attention even to the church, let him be like an unbeliever and a tax collector to you." (Matt. 18:15–17)

Notice there is a dispute between two members in a church. One has sinned against another. So Jesus tells the offended to try and be reconciled with the offender.

This kind of confrontation can be done poorly or well. Poorly, I recall hearing how Christine was offended when some of the members of her small group asked her challenging questions. So she left the study quietly hurt and angry. Weeks passed before she said anything. When she finally did, she didn't speak directly to the women who offended her but used the hurt to manipulate another woman in the group to her side. Her tone resonated with condemnation. Through it all, Christine was unwilling to consider the possibility that she was mistaken. The issue was never fully resolved.

Positively, I think of Cathy. Cathy was under a lot of stress at work. When her colleague and fellow church member Joey asked her to fulfill a task for which she was responsible, and which he was depending on, she snapped at him and refused. Gingerly and cautiously, Joey tried to approach her about the matter, but she immediately shut him down. Joey therefore spoke to another church member, Christopher, and asked him to intervene. Waiting for a calm moment, Christopher did. Cathy, melted by the Spirit and Christopher's loving words, immediately confessed and repented. Words of apology and a prayer of thanksgiving followed between the three of them.

Your job, Christian, is to work for reconciliation. Blessed are the peacemakers, for they will be called sons of God.

Restoration. It is also your job to work for restoration. Listen to how Paul puts it:

> Brothers, if someone is caught in any wrongdoing, you who are spiritual should restore such a person with a gentle spirit, watching out for yourselves so you also won't be tempted. Carry one another's burdens; in this way you will fulfill the law of Christ. (Gal. 6:1–2)

Jude envisions a similar situation when he exhorts, "save others by snatching them from the fire" (Jude 23). Both writers envision someone who is "caught." He or she is stuck. The legs are in quicksand. The hands are in shackles. The fire is all around, and so a restorer or rescuer is needed. That's you, if you are someone who is walking by the Spirit. But do it gently. And make sure you don't fall into the quicksand yourself.

Again, I can think of poor and positive examples of this. Poorly, James spoke with a flippant tone to Bart about his failures as a husband, provoking Bart's pride and shutting Bart's ears to the good counsel the James could have offered.

Positively, Liz knew she was unsympathetic with Jane's threat to leave her husband. So she forced herself to listen to Jane for an hour in order to understand and empathize with Jane's marital exasperation. Equipped with this empathy, she then had the ability to persuade Jane not to leave him. She talked Jane down and restored her.

Repentance. Your goal in discipline is to reconcile, to restore, and to encourage repentance. Listen to Paul again:

> It is widely reported that there is sexual immorality among you . . . a man is living with his father's wife. . . . I have already decided about the one who has done this thing as though I were present. When you are assembled in the name of our Lord Jesus with my spirit and with the power of our Lord Jesus, turn that one over to Satan for the destruction of the flesh, so that his spirit may be saved in the Day of the Lord. (1 Cor. 5:1, 4–5)

Paul had already decided about this individual: he was unrepentant. So Paul calls for immediate removal. There's no need for further conversation with the man. But that removal has a further purpose: repentance. The assembled Corinthians, as an embassy of Christ's kingdom, were to declare that the man was not one of their citizens, but a citizen of the kingdom of Satan. And the purpose: so that his spirit would be saved. The man was blind to his state, and he needed to repent.

Again, it's not difficult to think of poor and positive examples. Poorly, Lisa's pastors overlooked the fact that her parents were emotionally and borderline physically abusive toward her when they insisted the nineteen-year-old submit to her parents. After years of their controlling parenting, she moved out. When she described the harsh home circumstances to the elders, they accused her of not honoring her parents and trying to flee suffering, and proceeded to excommunication. No pastoral consideration was given to the pattern of abuse. (Years later the church apologized.)

Positively, my church excommunicated Quinn for unfaithfulness to his wife. The final step was taken after hours and hours of counseling work. In fact, the counseling continued off and on after the excommunication, including with the help of another church that Quinn tried to join, but who refused his admission until he worked out his business with us. Things went quiet for a while. Then Quinn showed up and subjected himself to several tough conversations with various elders and agreed to read a letter of confession and repentance before the whole church. The whole church agreed unanimously to re-extend the hand of fellowship to Quinn. Applause followed. He had repented.

After the Fact

What does your work look like after someone has been excluded from membership in a church? As we saw, Jesus requires, "let him be like an unbeliever . . . to you." Paul directs, "Do not even eat with such a person" (1 Cor. 5:11); and elsewhere "have nothing more to do with" a divisive person (Titus 3:10 ESV). So in one sense you must treat those who have been excommunicated like non-Christians. But they belong to a special category of non-Christian: they call themselves believers. Notice the context of Paul's direction:

> But now I am writing you not to associate with anyone who claims to be a believer who is sexually immoral or greedy, an idolater or verbally abusive, a drunkard or a swindler. Do not even eat with such a person. For what business is it of mine to judge outsiders? Don't you judge those who are inside? But God judges outsiders. (1 Cor. 5:11–13)

Paul expects for you to spend time with non-Christians who are sexually immoral, greedy, idolatrous, verbally abusive, drunk, and so forth. You might work with them. You might watch a game of football with them. The problem comes when an individual "claims to be a believer" and is "inside" the church. When such individuals are put "outside" the church, you should avoid casual interactions and fellowship.

Rather, your interactions should be marked by an uncomfortableness and awkwardness. No longer are you talking about weekend game scores. You're encouraging them to repent.

There are two important qualifications to make here. First, the elders of my church and I believe that someone who has been excommunicated can attend the church's public gatherings. After all, the public gathering includes the presence of non-Christians (see 1 Cor. 14). Plus, a church does not possess the power of the sword over a piece of geography. We cannot forcibly move people's bodies through physical space. Rather, a church possesses the power of the keys to make declarations, which it does by removing someone from membership and the Lord's Table. Therefore, our elders often tell the members of our church that there is no place we'd rather see the excommunicated person next Sunday than sitting under God's preached Word in church.

Second, the family members of an excommunicated individual should continue to fulfill family obligations to their excluded family member. Wives should continue to submit to husbands. Husbands should continue to love their wives. Children should honor their parents. Parents should still love their children. And so forth. These relationships are grounded in creation, not in the new covenant. The end of the church relationship, therefore, doesn't mean the end of the creation relationship. Of course, such relationships will require much wisdom. The wife of an excommunicated man, for instance, has a fine line to walk. She may share a Thanksgiving turkey with her husband, but she shouldn't ask him to lead the prayer.

The work of building relationships is sweet. The work of correcting sin and working for reconciliation, restoration, and repentance can be difficult. The work of walking away from an excommunicated member is, perhaps, the most difficult part of the work. When a sinner turns back from his sin, however, there is nothing better!

CHAPTER 5

A Description of Your Work—Part 2

In some ways, church discipline is about nothing more or less than assessing repentance. You shouldn't be surprised when Christians sin. The question is, do they repent? Once you establish that a person has sinned, that is the only question you are trying to answer.

Compare Dave and Pedro. Both struggled with drinking too much and could probably be labeled alcoholics. Both claimed they wanted to quit. Both tried to quit. Pedro did. Dave didn't. Or, he sort of did, then he didn't. Then did, then didn't. And so it went. Certainly Pedro was repentant. Was Dave? That's not always an easy question to answer.

I remember meeting almost weekly with Mike while he struggled with a pornography addiction. On a couple of occasions he went beyond pornography to meeting with women. Mike talked as if he hated his sin and generally seemed to be filled with remorse. But then he would pursue his sin again. In counseling Mike, I sometimes used the carrot of God's promises. Other times I would use the stick of God's warnings. Then carrot, then stick. Then anything else I could think of. I remember once sitting with Mike in a restaurant after the latest round of confessions. I sat dumbly, thinking to myself, "I have nothing to say. There's nothing else in my tool bag to help this guy!" I started to wonder if I should I bring in two or three others, or take it to the elders, and if it could go to the church.

Gratefully, I could see a couple of other patterns in Mike's life. First, the frequency with which he looked at pornography was decreasing—from seven days a week, to four days a week, to one day a week, and so on. Second, as long as I was in regular contact with Mike, he did better. When I got busy, he did worse. This encouraged me, ironically, because it suggested that the man was probably weaker than he was rebellious.

Paul tells us to account not just for the nature of the sin, but the nature of the sinner: "warn those who are irresponsible, comfort the discouraged, help the weak, be patient with everyone" (1 Thess. 5:14).

Ultimately, it seemed to me that Mike was repentant. I never took it further.

Two Kinds of Sorrow

Sometimes church members acknowledge they are in sin and refuse to budge. Sometimes they refuse to acknowledge they are in sin, such as in marital spats. Yet sometimes they admit they are wrong and promise to change. Your task then is to discern between godly sorry and worldly sorrow. Notice how Paul distinguishes between the two with the Corinthians:

> Now I rejoice . . . because your grief led to repentance. For
> you were grieved as God willed. . . . For godly grief produces
> a repentance not to be regretted and leading to salvation, but
> worldly grief produces death. For consider how much diligence
> this very thing—this grieving as God wills—has produced in
> you: what a desire to clear yourselves, what indignation, what
> fear, what deep longing, what zeal, what justice! In every way
> you showed yourselves to be pure in this matter. (2 Cor. 7:9–11)

Godly sorrow leads to change. It leads to a fight against sin. It will cut off the hand or gouge out the eye. It will typically receive your counsel—to meet at 6 a.m. for accountability; to offer the embarrassing confession; to join the group; to do whatever it takes to be done with the sin.

Worldly sorrow may genuinely feel bad. But you wonder if it feels bad for getting caught. Getting in trouble. After all, it excuses itself from taking the necessary measures to be done with the sin, or it only does the absolute minimum it can do to get out of trouble. There is not the indignation, fear, longing, and zeal that Paul describes. It drags its feet and slumps its shoulders like a five-year-old who is forced to obey but hangs onto his independence by pouting.

Worldly sorrow promises to change, but it doesn't really keep those promises. It's like the son in Jesus' parable who says he will work in the vineyard but then doesn't do it, as opposed to the son who says he won't work but then does. It's the second son who does the father's will, says Jesus, not the first (Matt. 21:28–31). A genuinely repentant person does God's will. A falsely repentant person does not.

So much of the wisdom we need in church discipline, whether private or public, is knowing how to distinguish worldly sorrow from godly sorrow. Godly sorrow is true repentance, and worldly sorrow is not. Again, the main question we're always asking in discipline is, are they repenting?

How Quickly Do You Move?

In fact, the pace of church discipline is pretty much entirely set by your or the church's ability to assess repentance. There are two paces for church discipline: slow and fast.

Slow. Matthew 18 provides the slow model. The circle starts as small as possible: one to one. Sin is not something that needs to be talked about broadly so it should be kept on a need-to-know basis. The circle expands only when the evidence suggests that the charges are legitimate and the person proves unrepentant. But the process moves slowly—weeks, even months.

Fast. First Corinthians 5 provides the fast model. Paul essentially begins where Matthew 18 ends. The whole church already knows about the man's sin. So there is no need to move slowly for that reason. And Paul has already judged the man as unrepentant (see v. 3). So there's no need to test the thesis and move slowly outward for that reason. Therefore Paul encourages the Corinthian church to remove the man immediately.

Sometimes theological writers in the past have remarked that the sin under consideration in 1 Corinthians 5 is a special kind of sin, namely, public and scandalous. And it's the sin's public and scandalous nature that requires the church to move quickly, giving no consideration to whether or not he's repentant. I don't think that's right. If your church determined that someone was genuinely repentant even of public and scandalous sin, it should not remove the person. You don't remove repentant people from the church—period. Now, the nature of some sins probably *should* prevent a church from thinking it's capable of assessing and affirming someone's repentance. Some scandalous sins might fall into this category. Suppose a man is caught in a pattern of grotesque sin that he has spent years lying about and covering up, such that, not only is he culpable for the sin, he has lived in gross hypocrisy all that time. Such a man may immediately apologize, even with tears, but a church in this situation may rightly determine that it is simply unable to affirm his apology as credible: "We *want* to believe you, but it would be irresponsible for us to continue confirming your public profession so quickly. You've given us too much cause to doubt your words." And therefore it removes him from membership, at least until his repentance from the sin, the deceit, and the hypocrisy is demonstrated over time.

I know of one church who found themselves in this situation. Only when he was arrested did the church became aware of a man's several years of predatory behavior toward women. Through prison bars he cried for forgiveness, but of course it was impossible for the church leaders to discern whether his tears were rooted in the worldly sorrow of public humiliation, or the godly sorrow of a genuine repentance. They rightly excommunicated him the following Sunday.

In short, 1 Corinthians 5 provides churches with the warrant to move toward excommunication quickly, even immediately, either when the church is confident beyond a reasonable doubt that an individual is unrepentant, or when the circumstances of the sin are such that it can no longer trust a person's mouthed words of repentance.

What does all this mean for you as an individual member? Your default setting should nearly always be to move slowly. God's Spirit does not always grant repentance in a torrential downpour, but sometimes in a slow gentle rain that gradually moistens the earth so that the seed of rebuke can take root and sprout over time. I recall discovering that a man was about to commit adultery. When I interrupted him, his first reaction was violent anger toward me. Within a day or two, he had adopted the posture of reluctant defeat. Within a week, his heart seemed to be genuinely broken for his treachery toward his wife.

Move slowly and give the benefit of the doubt. Fear God alone, so that you can speak challengingly. But always speak gently and peaceably.

When Do You Discipline?

The question of pace connects inevitably to the question of when to discipline or correct. I've labored since chapter 1 to emphasize the fact that the vast majority of discipline in a church should occur in the ordinary course of relationships on Monday to Saturday. This doesn't mean you want a church where the people run around correcting each other all the time. That sounds awful. It simply means that you want a church charac-

> "Iron sharpens iron, and one man sharpens another." (Prov. 27:17)

terized by people who hunger for godliness. Typically, members ask for correction, not hide from it, because they want to grow.

"Hey Ryan, do you have any feedback for me in how I led that meeting? What could I have done better?"

"Zach, I want you to know that you can always speak into my marriage and how you see me loving my wife. And, my flesh really doesn't want to ask this, but . . . any observations about how you've seen me parent?"

There's a reason, in other words, that writers sometimes distinguish between formative discipline and corrective discipline. Formative discipline means teaching. Corrective discipline means correcting mistakes. But obviously the two go hand in hand. It's hard to have one without the other. And in the life of the church, discipline as forming and correcting should characterize not just Sunday but Monday to Saturday. Discipline, you might say, is just another way of describing the discipleship process. When should discipleship and discipline occur? All week. That's when.

The harder question is, when do you take the process of discipline to the next level—from one to two or three, or from two or three to the whole church?

There is no easy formula here. Each case has to be judged on its own merits. I told you about Stephen in the last chapter. When he told me that God was "fine" with his sexual sin, it was clear to me that I should get another brother to join me. First, there was no dispute about Stephen's activity. We both agreed on what he was doing. Second, he was set in his ways. Our conversations (I think we had two by ourselves about the topic) were making no impression on him whatsoever. So I decided to involve Brad. Brad quickly found the same response and took it to the elders, who quickly found the same response and took it to the church. Frankly, this was one of the technically easier situations to deal with—even though heart-breaking—because the sin was so clear, so agreed upon, and so consciously unrepentant.

However, there have been other situations where our elders have labored for months, even years, with a troubled marriage or troubled individual, never deciding to take it to the next level. Again, this will be the case when the people involved are working with us to fight their sin. I remember our elder board working with one married couple over the course of four or five years, long enough that the elders who began the process of counseling the couple stepped off the board because their terms had expired. New elders stepped onto the board who had to be briefed on the situation, and this transition happened a couple of times during this couple's troubles. Neither of them was ever publicly excommunicated.

Here is a slightly easier question to answer, at least in theoretical terms: Which sins warrant public exposure and excommunication? An older generation of writers would often compile lists of sins from Scripture, such as those in 1 Corinthians 5 and 6, in order to answer that question: "Now I am writing you not to associate with anyone who claims to be a believer who is sexually immoral or greedy, an idolater or verbally abusive, a drunkard or a swindler" (1 Cor. 5:11). But if we just stick to those lists, does that mean we should excommunicate the greedy but not the embezzlers? The swindlers but not the murderers or pedophiles? Embezzlers, murderers, and pedophiles are never mentioned in these kinds of lists. In fact, I don't think we should treat these lists as exhaustive. Rather, Paul is describing the kind of sins we should expect to characterize people who remain unbelieving and unrepentant (see 1 Cor. 6:9–10).

I think the short answer to the above question is, only those sins which are *outward, significant,* and *unrepentant* warrant public exposure and excommunication. And a sin must be all three of those things, not just one or two of them.

> ### Which Sins?
>
> Which sins rise to the level of warranting excommunication? Sins that are simultaneously (1) outward, (2) significant, and (3) unrepentant.

1. A sin must be **outward**. It needs to be the kind of thing that you can see with the eyes or hear with the ears. It cannot be something that you suspect might be laying quietly within a person's heart. Paul lists greed in the list above, but you don't accuse someone of being greedy and then excommunicate him if you have no outward evidence for the greed. The secular court system is careful to weigh evidence. Should churches be any less careful? Jesus is not interested in mob justice. But notice I said "outward," not "public." Fornication, for instance, is not public. It's private. That's why I said "outward."

2. A sin must be **significant**. Anxiety and fear and stress might be sin. But I don't believe they warrant public exposure and excommunication. If I catch a brother embellishing a story, yet he denies it, he might be sinning. But I won't go public with it. Peter tells us that "love covers a multitude of sins" (1 Pet. 4:8). Surely one of the chief characteristics of a healthy church is a willingness to overlook many, even most, of the sins we experience at the hands of our fellow members. So what counts as significant sin? It's sin that makes it difficult for me to continue believing someone bears the Spirit of God and is a Christian, at least if he or she refuses to repent. Remember what membership is: a church's affirmation of a person's profession of faith. Significant sin is sin that makes it difficult, if not impossible, to stand before the watching world and continue to affirm a profession of faith as credible. I can with a clear conscience continue to affirm the faith of someone who denies he exaggerated a story; I cannot with a clear conscience do so for someone who persists in sexual immorality, verbal abuse, drunkenness, and so forth.

> "Love covers a multitude of sins."
> (1 Pet. 4:8)

Is the criteria for "significant" somewhat subjective? Yes, which is why the same sin in one situation may warrant excommunication while in another situation it might not, for a host of circumstantial factors. How easy it would be for Scripture to give us precise case law to deal with any and every conceivable situation. As it is, the Lord would have us appeal to him for wisdom and walk in faith. Incidentally, this is one more reason why churches should aspire to raise up as many elders as they can. You don't want one or two men having to weigh these difficult matters before bringing them to the church.

3. A sin must be **unrepentant.** The person has been confronted in his sin. And whether or not he acknowledges it is sin, and whether or not he says he will stop, he ultimately refuses

> "As a dog returns to its vomit, so a fool repeats his foolishness." (Prov. 26:11)

to let go of it; he keeps going back to it. He cannot (or will not) be separated from it, like a fool and his folly.

What Manner of Confrontation?

There were times when Jesus turned over tables in anger. There were times when the apostles spoke publicly with a sharp tongue toward particular individuals (think of Peter and Simon the magician in Acts 8; or Paul in 1 Corinthians 5). And there may be rare occasions when your correction of a fellow member must be a 9 or 10 on the severity scale.

But in the vast majority of circumstances, the manner of your confrontation or questioning should bear these characteristics:

- *Discrete:* the progression of Matthew 18 suggests that we should keep the circles as small as possible.
- *Gentle:* Paul tells us to restore people "with a spirit of gentleness" (Gal. 6:1 ESV).
- *Watchful:* In the same verse, Paul adds, "watch out for yourselves so you also won't be tempted." Jude agrees: "have mercy on others but with fear, hating even the garment defiled by the flesh" (v. 23). Sin is sneaky. It's easy to get caught even when you are trying to help others.

- *Merciful:* Jude says it twice: "have mercy" and "have mercy" (vv. 22–23). Your tone should be merciful and understanding, not self-righteous, as if you would never be susceptible to stumbling in the same way.
- *Impartial:* We should not pre-judge but work to hear both sides of the story (see 1 Tim. 5:21).
- *Clear:* Passive-aggressive or sarcastic confrontation is certainly out of order because it serves only to protect you. You should instead be willing to make yourself vulnerable by being very clear, especially if you are going to ask the person in sin to be vulnerable by confessing. At times understatement can serve the purposes of gentleness and help to draw a person out on their own. But this cannot compromise the purposes of clarity. The broader the circles become, the clearer you must be. After all, a little bit of yeast works through a whole batch of dough (1 Cor. 5:6). People must be warned.
- *Decisive:* Relatedly, when it comes to the final step of discipline—excommunication or exclusion—the action of the whole church must be decisive: "Clean out the old yeast so that you may be a new batch" (1 Cor. 5:7); "reject a divisive person" (Titus 3:10). It must be clear that the individual is no longer a church member or welcome to the Lord's Table.

Wisdom is always required in matters of correction, as discussed in chapter 2. No two situations are alike. It's easy to say, "Well, with this person, we did this." And there's much to be learned from precedent. But finally we must rely upon the principles of God's Word, the guidance of his Spirit, and a careful examination of the particulars and idiosyncrasies of every situation.

CHAPTER 6

Working with Others

The work of church discipline often brings two principles into apparent conflict. On the one hand, Matthew 18 recommends keeping the knowledge of a sin or dispute as small as possible. And think of all the biblical warnings against gossip. Gossip destroys relationships and escalates conflict:

> A gossip goes around revealing a secret, but a trustworthy
> person keeps a confidence. (Prov. 11:13)

> Whoever conceals an offense promotes love, but whoever gos-
> sips about it separates friends. (Prov. 17:9; 16:28)

> Without wood, fire goes out; without a gossip, conflict dies
> down. (Prov. 26:20)

So Proverbs explicitly says to "avoid someone with a big mouth" (20:19)! The New Testament presents gossip as one attribute of fallen humanity (Rom. 1:29; 2 Cor. 12:20).

On the other hand, Proverbs teaches there is wisdom in many counselors.

> Without guidance, people fall, but with many counselors there
> is deliverance. (Prov. 11:14)

> Plans fail when there is no counsel, but with many advisers
> they succeed. (Prov. 15:22)

So a crucial question becomes, how do we wisely solicit the help of others in the process of correction?

The larger issue at stake is knowing how to involve others wisely in the process of discipline. How do we seek counsel before confronting someone? How do we bring two or three others? When and how should we involve the elders? What is our role when something comes to the whole congregation?

Answering these questions is the burden of this chapter.

Getting Advice Beforehand

I remember one occasion in which I wanted to entreat a friend named Eric for the way I thought he had acted unkindly toward me. But I wasn't sure if my motives were correct. So I asked John whether I should speak to Eric. I didn't give John many of the details—only that Eric had offended me and I was bothered. I'm not entirely sure if it was right for me to consult with John, but the advice he gave was excellent: only confront Eric if your goal is to serve him.

That's the thing about talking to others first: you can get good counsel! But should you do it?

My best and not terribly profound answer to that question is . . . sometimes. It's probably ill-advised to speak to someone else first just because you are afraid. Fear God, not man. It's certainly ill-advised to speak to someone first because we want others to think less of the one who offended us. That's gossip. Sometimes we speak to others first because we suspect our own motives and want them to be checked, or because the conversation is politically precarious at any number of levels. Those *might* be good reasons to speak to someone else first.

Yet the key here is to consult others wisely and discretely. I knew John would be a good person to speak with because I knew he loved

Eric and my comments would not spoil his affection for or trust in Eric. Plus, I kept the details to an absolute minimum. I didn't tell him exactly what Eric did. Finally, I knew John was a spiritually mature man, a pastor in fact. Of course, all this was still just a judgment call, and I could have been wrong. A gossip separates friends, we saw above. Plus, a "gossip's words are like choice food that goes down to one's innermost being" (Prov. 18:8). Had I gone into detail, or had John been secretly harboring frustration with Eric himself, my words about Eric could have sunk deep down into John and further harmed his view of Eric.

Bringing One or Two Others

I think a similar set of principles apply when bringing one or two others, assuming we're following Jesus' recommended course in Matthew 18. You want people who are spiritually mature. You want people who—as best you can tell—know and love the person you are confronting. And you want to give them only the details they need to make a valid judgment.

For the purpose of helping them to be impartial, it's best to give the others just the facts, not your interpretation of the facts. There is a difference between "He was shouting at his kids" and "he was emotionally abusing his kids," if all you know is what you saw in a three-second window. There is a difference between "She says he forced himself on her" and "He forced himself on her," if all you know is what she told you. (Lawyers especially will tell you to be careful in potentially criminal situations to only report what you know.)

By the same token, you should avoid assessing people's hearts and motives. Of course this is true whether you're speaking one-on-one or to others. There's a difference between "He spoke crossly with me in front of the team" and "He spoke crossly with me because he wanted to make me look bad in front of the team."

One of the purposes for involving one or two others is that we should never fully trust ourselves. That is part of being a Christian—recognizing that we are prone to err and sin. And our desire for truth and justice should outweigh our sense that "Of course I'm right!" Involve one or two others only if you are willing for them to change your opinion. If you are unwilling, you may not be ready to begin the process.

Involving the Elders

There is no need for the one or two others to be elders. Ideally, in fact, they're not. Ideally, the person whom you mean to confront is plugged into the church and has a number of people around him who know and love him. If you are in a small group together, maybe you involve a third group member and the group leader. Assuming the sin can be taken care of right here, great! The group will be stronger, more loving, and more united for the experience.

But if the person has no relational ties, which, sadly, is too often the case, it may be best to bring in an elder or pastor at this second round of confrontation. This serves the purposes of discretion; and it takes advantage of any additional trust the individual may have toward someone in the office of elder (of course this might work in the opposite direction, too).

Certainly in situations where you and the one or two others find yourselves hitting a wall, you should go to the elders. God has given the elders or pastors oversight over the church to teach, warn, and admonish. They are shepherds and will give an account to God for every sheep within their care (Acts 20:28; Heb. 13:17). One of their main purposes as shepherds is to go after the one sheep who has wandered away from the ninety-nine. So involve them.

The Congregation

Our church discusses matters of discipline in closed-door meetings of the church only. When the Sunday evening service concludes, we say goodbye to guests and then resume our meeting. Ordinarily, the elders bring a matter of discipline to the whole church. No, Matthew 18 does not mention the idea of going through the elders. But there is no reason to read Matthew 18 apart from the texts of Scripture that give oversight over the whole church to the elders. Possessing oversight of the whole, they are both authorized and best equipped to know whether and how a case of discipline should go to the whole.

All that to say, if you have been involved in the preliminary stages of a discipline process, you can now follow the lead of the elders in bringing the situation to the attention of the whole church. For instance, they will best determine how much to tell the church, and you can follow their public cue in your private conversations.

How much information should pastors give the whole church? In general, I encourage pastors to name the category of sin, maybe a few details, and only details that are demonstrable and not debatable. There is no need to elaborate publicly on the whole saga of the sin. And it's best to avoid offering one's interpretations, as stated a moment ago. It's tempting for a pastor to give his interpretations, of course, because it allows him to use the emotionally weighty adjectives that seem so persuasive: "He was *awful*." The trouble is, interpretations are always debatable and therefore risk dividing the church. If the leaders do not have facts that can stand on their own, they should not bring the matter to the church.

Remember Paul's warning that a little bit of yeast works through the whole batch of dough, as well as his admonition not to even speak of what the evil do in secret. All this is cause for keeping the discussion of details to a minimum.

What if you haven't been involved in a process of discipline? You first hear of it when the elders bring the matter to the whole body. Can you discuss the discipline case with other members afterward? I would say, only sparingly. You can pray for the individuals involved. You might briefly mention your grief over the matter to a fellow member. And you might inform a member who was not in the meeting. But it's difficult to imagine what purpose discussing the matter at length with others might serve. Yes, the church should be warned about such sin. But the public communication of the sin in the context of discipline serves that purpose.

Not too long ago our elders informed the church that a man had left his wife and children for another woman. Several days later I was meeting with David, who is a younger man I disciple. Right before he got out of the car, David raised the discipline case. He told me that the situation had been heavy on his heart all week, and that he couldn't shake his grief. So we stopped and prayed that the wife and children would know God's comfort, that the man would repent, that the elders would lead with wisdom, and that the church would be protected from sin and disunity. That, I think, was a good conversation.

Finally, what do you do if you disagree with the recommendation for discipline made by the elders? Ordinarily, I would say you should only go against the recommendation of the pastors with great reluctance, particularly when it's reasonable to assume they know more about the situation than you. Scripture calls you to "submit" to them (Heb. 13:17). You have recognized these men as given by God to guide you in the way of biblical faithfulness simply by being a member of the church they shepherd. And if you only follow them in the places where you already know the way, are you really following?

That said, their authority over you is not final. God's is. And on the Last Day he will call you to account for how you employed your vote in every matter they bring before the church. God will ask, did you act according to what Scripture says? Were you faithful? It's not difficult to imagine that, on the Last Day, God will sometimes vindicate the decision to submit to the men God placed over us; and sometimes he will vindicate the decision to vote our conscience against the men he placed over us. Frustratingly (but purposefully, I think), the Bible offers no decision-making chart for determining when to do which. Instead, we must appeal to God for wisdom, and then act by faith.

People celebrate Martin Luther for appealing to conscience. In fact, I think we celebrate him because he was right in the things he was standing up for. Nobody celebrates the heretic Arius, who denied Jesus was God, even though he, too, presumably acted according to conscience. In other words, it's not enough to act according to your conscience, as if that is a get-out-of-jail-free card for excusing any bad decisions you might make. It's also important to be right. Scripture is the surest guide for being right. Yet Jesus also gives us pastors or elders to lead us in the way of Scripture.

Other Churches

Is one church bound by another church's disciplinary decisions? As a congregationalist, I believe that the answer to that, formally, is no. Informally, however, yes, churches should work together. On a couple of occasions now, my church has excommunicated individuals who began attending other churches, and those churches have told the individuals they needed to be reconciled with my church before they joined their churches. And then those churches worked with our pastors in counseling the individual through the steps of repentance. These other churches were not required by Scripture to do this as a matter of proper church polity. But they were wise to do so. It showed love for the individual excluded by my church, and for my church.

On another occasion, a woman attempted to join our church who had been excommunicated by another church. After speaking at length to the woman, her husband, and her former pastors, our elders decided that her previous church was in error and so recommended her membership to our congregation. We believed they had acted in an authoritarian manner.

So formally, churches do not bind one another. Informally, they do well to work together when a matter of discipline spreads across more than one congregation.

What does that mean for you as a church member? If more than one church is involved, do your best to follow the counsel of your elders.

The Whole Church

Church discipline, finally, is a ministry of the whole church. It begins formatively in the pulpit when the preacher preaches. His biblical words correct our false thinking and living. Discipline continues as we speak God's Word to one another with psalms, hymns, and spiritual songs. How easily our affections and emotions go astray, which the songs work to correct. The discipline then works through our conversations with each other after the service and into the week. This happens as we encourage, instruct, warn, and admonish one another according to God's Word.

Failing to practice church discipline undermines the call to repentance by the preacher. It undermines a congregation's belief in the lordship of Christ. And it works against the church's ability to embrace a robust, life-changing gospel and the call to holiness. The famous nineteenth-century Baptist theologian J. L. Dagg once observed, "When discipline leaves a church Christ goes with it."[2]

There is a reason that God says his discipline "produces a harvest of righteousness and peace for those who have been trained by it" (Heb. 12:11 NIV). Instead of rolling fields of golden wheat, you can envision rolling fields of righteousness and peace. What must that look like?!

It looks like the members of a church living in harmony and holiness, having been trained by discipline.

CHAPTER 7

Abuses of the Work

By God's grace, I don't have any firsthand stories to tell from my church experience about an abusive example of church discipline. Perhaps God will inform me otherwise on the Last Day. After all, many abusive churches probably testify the same thing. Yet so far as I am aware, I have none to offer.

No credit to me in that. I have been privileged to serve as an elder with godly, humble, and careful men. Only recently, in fact, we were discussing a woman's resignation, and I argued that we should withhold her resignation and move toward discipline. Later events, however, suggested that I was probably mistaken. Gratefully, I was in the minority when our elders voted on the matter that night.

The work, to be sure, is difficult, requiring more wisdom than any one of us have. I remember another occasion when the elders were considering whether or not to restore someone whom the church had excommunicated for substance abuse. He was showing new signs of fighting his addiction, yet he remained somewhat ornery and combative with us, and he refused to reengage with his wife since his outside counselor told him it would interrupt his recovery. As we discussed the matter, most of us felt divided, and I probably changed my mind four times in the course of the conversation, depending on who spoke last (see Prov. 18:17). When the vote came for restoration, 7 voted against restoration and 6 voted for. Later history affirmed the 7, but at the time we all felt the heaviness and difficulty of the moment. We didn't like making such a significant decision by this bare majority, but, still, we trusted God's guidance through the majority. He had appointed all of us together to make even these tough, unclear decisions.

The takeaway lesson I would offer from this story is, most church discipline situations are ethically, spiritually, and pastorally complicated, and so we should be very slow to condemn our leaders or other churches. The media is quick to scream fire at the faintest smell of smoke. But we should not be so quick. Have you ever sat at a decision-making table, stared at all the facts, struggled with everyone else at the table to find the best path forward, prayed hard, made the best decision you could, and then had a chorus of critics who questioned your decision though they knew but a fraction of the facts that you knew? Yes, leaders need accountability. Still, we must be very slow to judge the decisions of others when we don't see everything they see.

That said . . .

Characteristics and Causes of Churches That Abuse

Churches should work hard against the possibility of abusive church discipline, and we should act quickly against it! In my writing and speaking on this topic, most of the churches I address suffer from complacency and laxity in discipline. A few, however, approach it too stridently.

Anecdotally, most (or all?) of the unfortunate cases of church discipline I have heard about in recent years have occurred in non-congregational churches, where the elders are free to impose their will on the congregation. I'm sure congregational churches have failed in this area as well. But the mere fact that a group of elders or pastors in a congregational church must sit in a small elders' meeting before the big congregational meeting, scratch their heads, and ask themselves, "How are we going to explain this to the church?" tends by itself to moderate their decision making. It slows them down. A group of well-meaning but tired elders might get highjacked by a bad strain of thinking in their meeting at 10 p.m. on a Thursday night. But Sunday's congregational meeting will serve as a useful reality check.

In my observations, wrong approaches to discipline can occur in large churches when the sheer size impels them to rely on regulated processes instead of personal pastoral care. The need for economies of scale is met with consistent and tidy procedures and precise codes of conduct. Treating each case uniquely and thoughtfully becomes difficult. Yet just as a wise parent treats each child individually, so wise discipline treats each member individually. From personal experience, I can say that disciplining and training my children is slow, inefficient work that consumes hours. And so is the work of disciplining and training our fellow members.

Abuse seems more common among churches and church leaders who are uncomfortable with theological and practical tensions, tensions that I believe are inevitable in a fallen world. A fundamentalist mind-set, I've remarked in other writings, prefers things in black and white. It takes one principle and makes it ultimate, instead of letting that one principle be tempered by competing principles. For instance, there's a tension between not gossiping and getting outside counsel before confronting someone, as described at the beginning of chapter 6.

An egregious example of the fundamentalist error occurs in churches with a strong concept of male headship and parental authority. These are biblical principles that I entirely affirm. Yet I've been angered to hear of churches where the elders, in the name of respecting headship, condone or at least overlook reports of husbands who are harsh, severe, and demanding with their wives. They've let one principle become too dominant, uninformed by other biblical principles.

In general, you should be leery of joining a church where the leaders play favorites, punish those who disagree, have a temper, use the silent treatment, must always have the last word, cannot be wrong, emphasize external conformity, are consistently dogmatic on both the big and small issues, seldom if ever admit they are wrong, have difficulty giving authority to others, only promote their closest friends or family members, and generally need control. You can probably think of more yellow flags. You might even look for a few in yourself. Personally, I like to have the last word. That's not a good sign for my use of authority. I better trust the authority of the man who is willing to give another person the last word. He's less concerned about appearances or forcing outcomes. Speaking of which . . .

It's commonplace that abusive authority roots in pride. But another way of putting this, I think, is to say that abusive authority and discipline root in "fear of man." A person who fears God more than anything is less likely to abuse God's subjects. But a person who fears man cares too much about appearances. He or she needs control over the façade of things.

The most tyrannical rulers in the home, state, or church are the insecure and fearful ones. Please do not place me under a leader who lives in fear.

A man or a church who says, "He must increase, but I must decrease," is far less likely to abuse authority and discipline. The man or the church who is always trying to "increase" is more likely to abuse it.

Perhaps the most vivid and damnable form of spiritual abuse on the pages of the New Testament, besides the false teachers who would mislead a flock, is the legalistic religion of the Pharisees and the teachers of the law. They impose laws where God imposes none. They condemn others for the sake of their own gain. They lord it over others so that they might be honored. And finally they are willing to kill God himself for the sake of maintaining control.

Cultivating the Right Culture

The best way to avoid an abusive church culture where discipline is pursued harshly is nothing other than the gospel and working to cultivate a gospel culture.

I once had the opportunity to address a number of the elders of a church who handled a terribly complex case of church discipline piously but poorly. The media had picked up on the story, and a number of writers, Christian and non-Christian, charged the church with abusiveness. In fact, I know the church and its leaders, and it is a gospel-centered and healthy church. The brothers made a mistake in a complicated situation, a mistake for which they quickly apologized and altered course.

Good churches will make mistakes, just like good parents and good presidents will make mistakes. Name one famous leader in the Bible who didn't—Abraham? Moses? David? Solomon? Jesus knows this. And he knew it when he granted each of these institutions mediating authority. The fact that even our best leaders make mistakes helps us to put our final hope in Christ, the only mistake-less leader.

So let's assume that mistakes, even sinful mistakes, will happen. The question is, what's the best environment for absorbing the harmful effects of those mistakes? And what's the best environment for preventing mistakes? The answer must be, a gospel environment. The brothers in the church just mentioned were able to apologize and reverse course as quickly as they did because they know and live by the gospel. They have no image to defend, no life or decision-making pattern to justify. They are justified in Christ, which frees them to apologize quickly.

And, ironically, I think the healthier church just might be the one where the leaders make mistakes and apologize for them than the church where the leaders seem never to make mistakes or apologize.

This is a lesson I have had to learn in parenting. Suppose you have two parents: the parent who maintains excellent external appearances and so never perceives his or her need to ask for forgiveness, and the parent who sins, both against the children and otherwise, but who is quick to ask for forgiveness and live transparently in the gospel. Which is the better parent? Which, that is, will do a better job of shepherding his or her children down a gospel path?

In the early years of parenting, I was more the first parent. I generally kept up good appearances, and I found it difficult to apologize or admit mistakes to my daughters when my conscience suggested I might. After all, I wanted to give them a good model to look up to. I didn't want to spoil their image of me by admitting weakness. And at times—tragically—they said that they thought I never sinned. What an anti-gospel lesson I had been teaching! Oh, girls, if you only knew the pride and selfishness of your father's heart.

Churches and their leaders, too, must learn to live transparently in the gospel, meaning we confess our sins to one another and rejoice in the grace that God gives. The witness of these embassies of Christ's kingdom does not depend upon our moral perfection. How attractive is a building full of Pharisees? Rather, our international witness depends upon our gospel love and forgiveness amidst the sin that remains.

> "I give you a new command: Love one another. Just as I have loved you, you must also love one another. By this all people will know that you are My disciples, if you have love for one another." (John 13:34–35)

What does it mean to love one another as Christ has loved us? It means loving mercifully and forgivingly. And of course doing that means confessing our sin to one another so that we can be forgiven. This is how you live transparently in the gospel. And it's this kind of corporate life together that shows the world that we are his disciples.

Notice then who it is that churches excommunicate: they excommunicate the Pharisees. Pharisees are the ones who never acknowledge their sin as sin, and so never repent of it. Of course I'm using the word Pharisees a little more broadly than you might be accustomed to. You're probably thinking of the Pharisees about whom we read in the Gospels who kept the law "perfectly." What I'm saying here is, they are of the same breed as the so-called wayward sinner who refuses to let go of his sin. Neither is poor in spirit. Neither will confess. Both will justify themselves to the very end. Both, in other words, are legalists. And the successful legalist and the failed legalist are both legalists, both "Pharisees." Church discipline, done wisely, is nothing other than a device for striking against Pharisaism in the church. Not only do the Pharisees refuse to see the planks in their own eyes, they refuse to let others point out the specks.

Ironically, it's the people who eschew all church discipline that might be the biggest Pharisees of all because they cannot imagine themselves being self-deceived or in need of correction: "How dare you call out the speck in my eye!" The poor in spirit, the meek, and the lovers of the gospel, however, both acknowledge their planks and welcome those who might point out the specks.

> Don't rebuke a mocker, or he will hate you; rebuke a wise man,
> and he will love you. (Prov. 9:8)

In which home or church would you prefer to live—the one where everyone is "perfect"? Or the one where people confess their sin and live trusting in the vicarious righteousness of Christ? If the latter, do you take the initiative, not in correcting others, but in confessing your sin? If not, could it be that *you* are the one who is more likely to pursue church discipline abusively?

Moving forward, know that confession is a necessary prerequisite for correction, and that the person who cannot be corrected probably doesn't know how to confess either.

Gospel Courage and Fear of Man

The Old Testament book of Joshua has much to teach about church discipline. Joshua and the people enter the Promised Land of Canaan, destroy the inhabitants, and establish cities for the praise of God's name. The whole nation of Israel was to be an Old Testament rendition of God's embassy on earth. It existed to broadcast a heavenly justice and righteousness among the nations. Therefore, God took pains to ensure that his people remained holy. For instance, he judged Achan for stealing the spoils of war against Jericho.

One of the more famous lines in the book of Joshua must be God's charge to Joshua to be strong and courageous upon entering the land. Three times he says it:

> **"Be strong and courageous,** for you will distribute the land I swore to their fathers to give them as an inheritance. Above all, **be strong and very courageous** to carefully observe the whole instruction My servant Moses commanded you. . . . Haven't I commanded you: **be strong and courageous**? Do not be afraid or discouraged, for the Lord your God is with you wherever you go." (Josh. 1:6–7, 9, emphasis added)

Joshua was to be strong and courageous as he took over the land. He was to be strong and courageous in obeying God's instruction. And he was to be strong and courageous knowing the Lord was with him.

In chapter 2 I argued that church discipline requires a commitment to the gospel, a longing for God's holiness, godly love, a commitment to biblical freedom, and wisdom. Now let me add one more thing: it requires strength and courage. Correcting another person, particularly in the all-accepting, intolerantly tolerant West of today, requires strength and courage. This is true informally and interpersonally. This is true formally and publicly.

People who live in fear either never correct others or they correct others too harshly. They fall into one ditch or the other—silence or severity. After all, both the silent and the severe worry about their reputations, and losing control, and unforeseen consequences. Therefore they do everything they can to avoid making waves, or they try to control the room. And to be sure, in defense of the first group, there is wisdom in staying clear of trouble: "A person who is passing by and meddles in a quarrel that's not his is like one who grabs a dog by the ears" (Prov. 26:17).

That said, there is a time and season for everything, including a time to rescue a brother or sister in Christ from their sin. It's not only the wise who can best judge the time; it's the strong and courageous. Strong, God-fearing leaders and Christians don't react to threats. They don't panic. They don't feel compelled to force circumstances or hearts that cannot be compelled. Rather, their courage leaves them free to assess a situation more objectively and carefully—to be wise.

The fear of the Lord, therefore, is not only the beginning of wisdom, as Proverbs says (1:7). It's the beginning of church discipline. When you fear God rightly, you prize holiness rightly, and you are strong and courageous before the toothless threats of sin and sinners. You know God will be with you as you obey his instruction and seek to conquer his territory.

So don't give me pastors or church members where people are afraid of one another, the media, the raised eyebrows of the Pharisees, or even of me. Give me pastors and church members who fear the Lord. It's there I will be safest. And I pray for you, dear reader, that you will be strong and courageous.

NOTES

1. Henry Drummond, *The Greatest Thing in the World* (Grand Rapids, MI: Revell, 1911).

2. J. L. Dagg, *A Treatise on Church Order* (Charleston, SC: The Southern Baptist Publication Society, 1858), 274.

SCRIPTURE INDEX